JUNIOR SONGSCAPE

THE ULTIMATE SONGBOOK FOR CLASSROOM AND CONCERT USE

LIN MARSH

with CD

132 St. Pancras Way,
London NW1 9NB

Tel: 020-7482-5424
Fax: 020-7482-5434
E-mail: dot@dotsonline.co.uk
Web: www.dotsonline.co.uk

FABER *ff* MUSIC

20·25

ACKNOWLEDGEMENTS

I would like to thank Codj Black, Shirley Court, Lis Fletcher, Wendy Reynolds, Janet Wheeler and Janet Mills, who commissioned various songs contained in *Junior Songscape*. Thanks also to Dominic Marsh and Kathryn Oswald, who sang along with me on the CD recording – and, of course, to John for making the tea!

Lin Marsh

CD recorded in Chestnut Studio, Oxon, 21 February & 19 March, 2002
Produced by Kathryn Oswald and Leigh Rumsey
Engineered by Mike Skeet, skeetmusic.com
℗ 2002 Faber Music Ltd © Faber Music Ltd

Singers: [1] Lin Marsh; [2] Dominic Marsh; [3] Kathryn Oswald
Piano: Lin Marsh

To buy Faber Music publications or to find out about the full range of titles available please contact your local music retailer or Faber Music sales enquiries:

Faber Music Limited, Burnt Mill, Elizabeth Way, Harlow, CM20 2HX England
Tel: +44 (0)1279 82 89 82   Fax: +44 (0)1279 82 89 83
sales@fabermusic.com   www.fabermusic.com

PREFACE

Junior Songscape is an exciting collection of songs suitable for use with singers in the 5 to 11 age group. It is a book to be dipped into for concerts, class singing or assemblies, and contains many new songs as well as some old favourites. All the songs are appropriate for young singers in content and vocal range. There are songs about seasons, feelings, history, travel and Shakespeare's *Macbeth* and *Julius Caesar*, and songs from musical theatre. There are several rounds to encourage part-singing, and harmony parts (many of which are optional) in other songs for those who are more confident.

Keyboard accompaniments have been left deliberately simple, and chord symbols for guitarists are included. The CD provides complete performances of all the songs to ease learning: when more confident, adjust the right and left balance so that you can sing and work along to the accompaniment alone. The rounds provide just the keyboard accompaniments, giving you the flexibility to choose how you wish to perform them.

There are many ways to sing rounds: I often let each part repeat the last line until the last group has finished singing – this way that last little group feels supported. When teaching simple part-songs, it can be a good idea to let one half hum their part quietly, helping the others –

who are learning a new bit – to keep in time and give them a sense of key. It also keeps them all occupied! You may find pupils who would like to sing a solo verse or sing in a small group. Do encourage them to do this – it is great for confidence, and often very effective for a first verse.

Always find time in your singing session to warm up the voices. This will focus the mind on the work, make pupils aware of posture and support, and get voices moving. Work lips and tongue in some tongue-twisters or imagine chewing gum with big mouths!

Movement often enhances a performance but needs to be simple and effective. If you are going to add actions, take ideas from the children. They may even like to devise their own choreography! For ideas and suggestions for warm ups and movement, have a look at *The show must go on!* (Lin Marsh and Wendy Cook, Faber Music).

The intention of this book is to provide singing repertoire that will encourage pupils to sing with joy and confidence. Commitment to the music and the words should bring out real communication skills and enable your singers to give a thrilling and expressive performance. And when you've explored all the songs in this collection, why not try *Songscape, Key Stage 3*?!

Lin Marsh, April 2002

CONTENTS

Orange and yellow and brown

Lin Marsh

Summer holiday

from Summer holiday

Words and music by
Bruce Welch and Brian Bennett
arr. Lin Marsh

Listen to the rain

Summer

Lin Marsh

MELODY

In an easy manner ♩ = 114

mp

1: Ear - ly morn - ing

PIANO/
KEYBOARD

Dmaj⁷

mp

light
fall - ing on my win - dow,
(2) flowers,
co - lours all a - round me,
(3) beach,
days of fun and laugh - ter,

Em/D

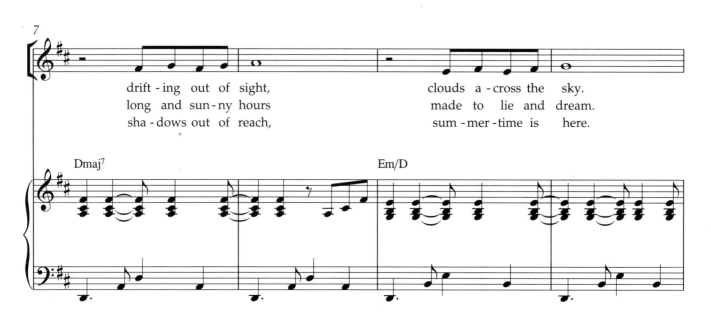

drift - ing out of sight,
clouds a - cross the sky.
long and sun - ny hours
made to lie and dream.
sha - dows out of reach,
sum - mer - time is here.

Dmaj⁷

Em/D

catch the break-ing waves as they race a-cross the sand,

catch the sum-mer breeze as it wan-ders warm and

free and save a lit-tle sun-shine just for

me.

2: Gar-dens full of

3: Peo-ple on a

Carry the corn

Lin Marsh

No matter what

from *Whistle down the wind*

Music by Andrew Lloyd Webber
Words by Jim Steinman
arr. Lin Marsh

Do you know how it feels?

Lin Marsh

Over the rainbow

from *The Wizard of Oz*

Music by Harold Arlen
Words by E. Y. Harburg
arr. Lin Marsh

22

Consider yourself

from Oliver!

Words and Music by
Lionel Bart
arr. Lin Marsh

With vigour ♩. = 112

MELODY

mf

PIANO/KEYBOARD

mf

D⁷   G♯dim   D⁷   Con -

-si - der your - self   at   home,_____ con - si - der your-self
-si - der your - self   well   in,_____ con - si - der your-self

G

one of the fa - mi - ly.   We've ta - ken to you   so
part of the fur - ni - ture. There is - n't a lot   to

E⁷/G♯   Am   D⁷   G   B/F♯

strong,   it's clear   we're   go - ing to get a - long. Con -
spare.   Who cares?   What   -ev - er we've got we

1.

Em   E♯dim   D/F♯   D♯dim   Em   A⁷   D   D⁷

24

Singing in the bath

Lin Marsh

Tomorrow

from Annie

Words by Martin Charnin
Music by Charles Strouse
arr. Lin Marsh

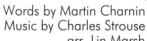

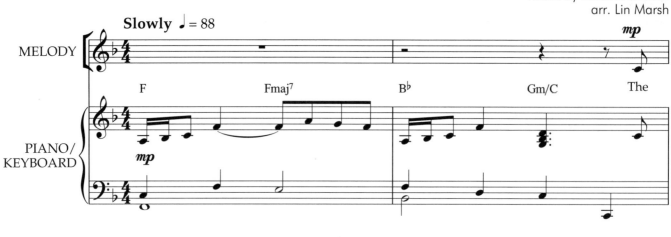

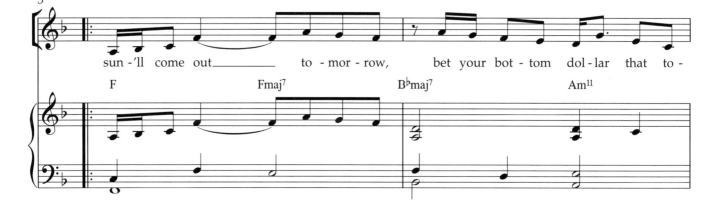

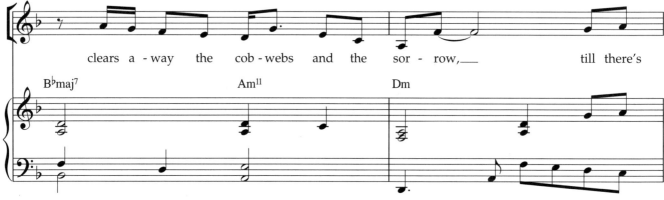

Thank you for the music

Words and Music by
Benny Andersson and Björn Ulvaeus
arr. Lin Marsh

*Alternative words

The disco beat

Lin Marsh

Whistle down the wind

from *Whistle down the wind*

Music by Andrew Lloyd Webber
Words by Jim Steinman
arr. Lin Marsh

The last dinosaur

Lin Marsh

Man and horse

Lin Marsh

Lyrics:

1: Man and horse, who'd have guessed this would be a
2: Years passed by, then with pride man dis - co - vered
3: Man and horse, what an act, came to make a

great suc - cess? Man and horse, what a pair! Found they had so
he could ride. Learnt to jump, learnt to trot, both seemed hap - py
life - long pact. Man and horse, what a dream, made a most ef -

much to share.___ Man knew just what
with their lot.___ Put a sad - dle
-fect - ive team.___ Pull - ing ploughs and

Any dream will do

from *Joseph and the Amazing Technicolor Dreamcoat*

Music by Andrew Lloyd Webber
Words by Tim Rice
arr. Lin Marsh

46

Camelot

Lin Marsh

Turn on your video

Lin Marsh

last time to Coda

are there up-on your screen with a vi-de-o,_____ watch it go.___

E^7sus^4 E^7 Am   F   C/G Dm^7/G

mp

1: We would like to tra-vel to a
2: We have al-ways longed to see the
3: Could you face the pe-rils of a

C   G/C

mp

place that's far a-way, see the an-cient sights of
crea-tures of the deep, and the a-ni-mals who
jour-ney back in time? From the migh-ty Bron-to-

F/C   C

A-thens or the traf-fic in L. A. We could
wake to play when we are fast a-sleep. We would
-sau-rus to Vic-to-ria in her prime. Climb a-

G/C   F/C   C

mf

mf

Spare the rod

Lin Marsh

* bb, 15–18 can also stand alone as a round.

Stars, hide your fires

Lin Marsh

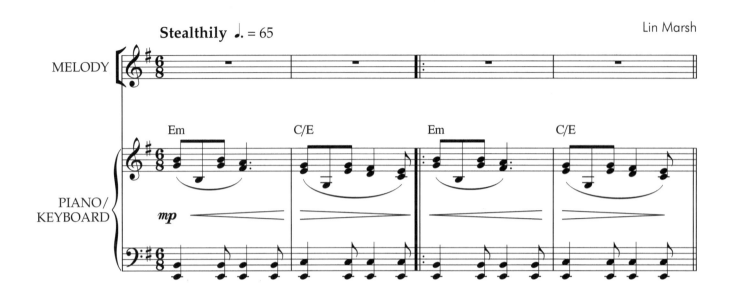

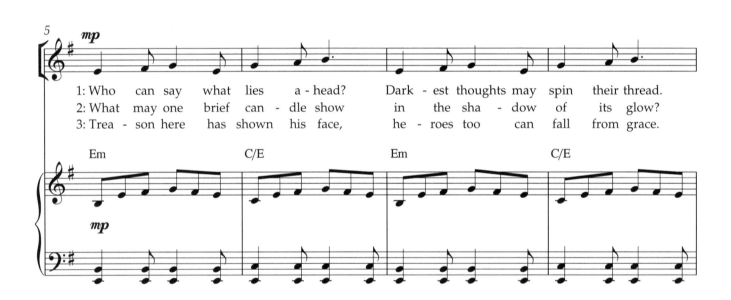

1: Who can say what lies a - head? Dark - est thoughts may spin their thread.
2: What may one brief can - dle show in the sha - dow of its glow?
3: Trea - son here has shown his face, he - roes too can fall from grace.

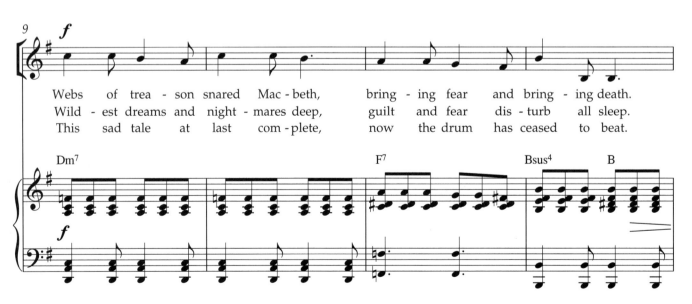

Webs of trea - son snared Mac - beth, bring - ing fear and bring - ing death.
Wild - est dreams and night - mares deep, guilt and fear dis - turb all sleep.
This sad tale at last com - plete, now the drum has ceased to beat.

Beware the Ides of March

Lin Marsh

Cae - sar tries to sleep.
Cae - sar's heart is stilled.

2: Be -

3: Feel the earth is tremb - ling and groan - ing, see the graves have yield - ed their dead.

Hear the migh - ty wind is a - moan - ing, shoot - ing stars to hea - ven have fled!

4: Be -

Gently the river

(Round)

With gentle movement ♩ = 105

Lin Marsh

Rush-hour round

Lin Marsh

* last time

Wheels!

Lin Marsh

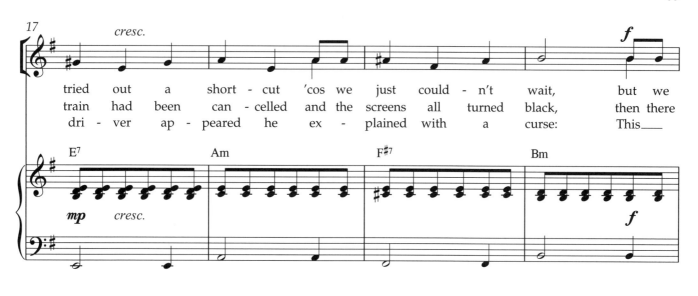

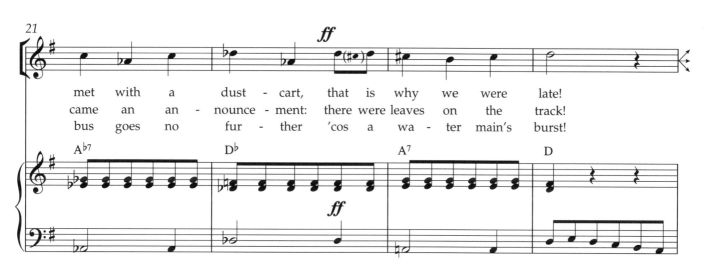

64

Grand canals

Lin Marsh

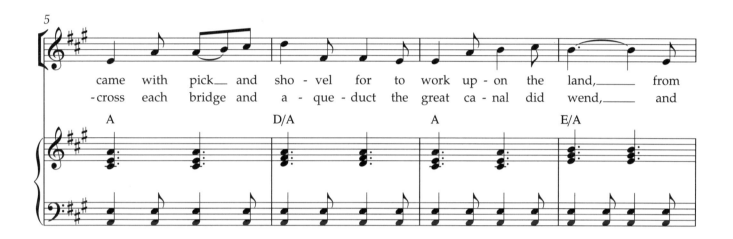

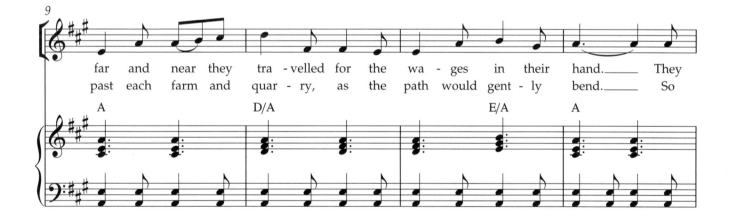

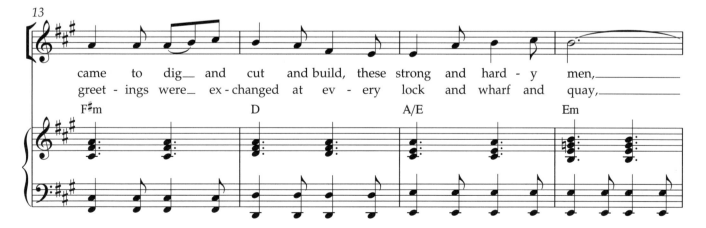

68

Rocking
(Round)

Lin Marsh

Steam train

Lin Marsh

*Try taking v.5 at a faster speed through to the end!

© 2002 by Faber Music Ltd.

LYRICS

Orange and yellow and brown
See the leaves are falling,
autumn days are calling,
Orange and yellow and brown,
orange and yellow and brown.

Fields and pastures all are bare,
autumn colours ev'rywhere,
Orange and yellow and brown …

Cattle grazed and corn grew high
in the summer sun,
flowers and blossom sang their song,
now their work is done.

Morning mist now chills the air,
golden tree tops ev'rywhere,
Orange and yellow and brown …

Summer holiday
We're all going on a summer holiday,
no more working for a week or two.
Fun and laughter on our summer holiday,
no more worries for me or you
for a week or two.

1 | We're going where the sun shines brightly,
we're going where the sea is blue.
We've seen it in the movies,
now let's see if it's true.

2 | Sun shines brightly, sea is blue,
seen the movies, is it true?

Ev'rybody has a summer holiday,
doin' things they always wanted to,
so we're going on a summer holiday
to make our dreams come true
for me and you.

Listen to the rain
Listen to the rain
  falling on my window,
listen to the rain
  splashing on the ground.
Listen to the rain
  thund'ring on the rooftops,
  beating on the door and making
  puddles all around.

Listen to the rain,
  still no sign of stopping,
faster still it pours
  down my window pane.
Rainy, rainy day,
  never-ending showers,
  fetch your boots and your umbrella,
  here it comes again!

Listen to the rain –
  hasn't stopped for days now,
grey skies all around,
  not a patch of blue.
On and on it falls,
  filling up the rivers,
  rising higher by the minute,
  what are we to do?

Summer
Early morning light
falling on my window,
drifting out of sight,
clouds across the sky.
Hours and hours of lazing in the sun,
time to spend in simply having fun
till day is done.
  Catch the summer sun
  and hold it in your hand,
  catch the breaking waves
  as they race across the sand,
  catch the summer breeze
  as it wanders warm and free
  and save a little sunshine just for me.

Gardens full of flowers,
colours all around me,
long and sunny hours
made to lie and dream.
Butterfly don't wish your life away,
share with me the beauty of today,
why can't you stay?
  Catch the summer sun …

People on a beach,
days of fun and laughter,
shadows out of reach,
summertime is here.
How I wish this magic spell would stay,
brightening the year from day to day
in summer's way.
  Catch the summer sun …

Carry the corn
The summer is over, September is here,
there's a chill in the morning, the air cool and clear.
We've gathered together our harvest to share
and we'll bring it all home while the weather is fair.
  There's Ned and there's Dobbin,
  there's Jack and there's Joe,
  they're fed and they're watered and ready to go.
Each team now is harnessed and waits to begin,
and they'll carry the corn, carry the corn,
carry the corn till it's all gathered in.

The fields stand so golden, the sun rising high,
a last lonely swallow appears in the sky.
The wagons are loaded with many a song,
while the great shire horses stand steady and strong.
  There's Ned and there's Dobbin …
They'll toil and they'll labour beneath the bright sun,
and they'll carry the corn, carry the corn,
carry the corn till the work is all done.

Our bodies are aching as homeward we go,
the sun's slowly setting, the fields are a-glow.
With jingle of harness and many a smile,
we walk with the horses the last weary mile.
  There's Ned and there's Dobbin …
What strength and devotion, such friendship they've shown
and they'll carry the corn, carry the corn,
carry the corn till the harvest is home.

No matter what
No matter what they tell us,
no matter what they do,
no matter what they teach us,
what we believe is true.
No matter what they call us,
however they attack,
no matter where they take us,
we'll find our own way back.
I can't deny what I believe,
I can't be what I'm not,
I know our love's for ever,
I know, no matter what.

If only tears were laughter,
if only night was day,
if only prayers were answered,
then we would hear God say:
'No matter what they tell you,
no matter what they do,
no matter what they teach you,
what you believe is true.
And I will keep you safe and strong
and sheltered from the storm,
no matter where it's barren,
our dream is being born.'

No matter who they follow,
no matter where they lead,
no matter how they judge us,
I'll be ev'ryone you need.
No matter if the sun don't shine,
or if the skies are blue,
no matter what the ending,
my life began with you.
I can't deny what I believe,
I can't be what I'm not,
I know this love's for ever,
that's all that matters now
  no matter what.

Do you know how it feels?
Do you know how it feels when you're waiting for tomorrow?
Do you know how it feels when there's something in the air?
Perhaps something special you're hoping might happen,
or maybe a secret at last you can share.
  And you just can't wait, can't wait until tomorrow,
  you just can't wait, you're counting ev'ry day.
  You're feeling impatient, so very excited,
  yet still that special moment seems so very far away.

Do you know how it feels when the minutes go so slowly?
Do you know how it feels when each day seems like a year?
You long for this moment with all of your being,
you're holding your breath for it soon may be here.
  And you just can't wait …

Over the rainbow
Somewhere over the rainbow
  way up high,
there's a land that I heard of once
  in a lullaby.
Somewhere over the rainbow
  skies are blue
and the dreams that you dare to dream
  really do come true.

Some day I'll wish upon a star
and wake up where the clouds are far
  behind me,
Where troubles melt like lemon drops
away above the chimney pots that's where
  you'll find me.
Somewhere over the rainbow
  blue birds fly,
Birds fly over the rainbow,
  why then, oh why can't I?

Some day I'll wish upon a star …

Consider yourself
  Consider yourself at home,
  consider yourself one of the family.
  We've taken to you so strong,
  it's clear we're going to get along.
  Consider yourself well in,
  consider yourself part of the furniture.
  There isn't a lot to spare.
  Who cares? Whatever we've got we share.

If it should chance to be we should see some harder days,
empty larder days, why grouse?
Always a chance we'll meet somebody to foot the bill,
then the drinks are on the house!
  Consider yourself our mate,
  we don't want to have no fuss,
  for after some consideration we can state,
  Consider yourself one of us!

Consider yourself at home …

Nobody tries to be lah-di-dah and uppity,
there's a cup of tea for all.
Only it's wise to be handy wiv' a rolling pin
when the landlord comes to call!
  Consider yourself our mate …

Singing in the bath
Singing in the bath is such a lovely thing to do,
shut the bathroom door and you're a star!
Nobody will hear you when the water starts to flow,
  first a little exercise:
  La la la la la la la la la,
add your alpine bath-oil and breathe the mountain air,
  Yodel eedle, idle odle ay,
  Sing it under water *blll*
and wash those worries away.

Singing in the bath will make you feel so good inside,
take a breath and see what you can do.
How about a pop-star who is singing on T.V.?
  Just pick up your microphone:
  Shoobady doobady doobady doo,
when you feel dramatic, an opera's the thing,
  Piano, Pavarotti, e forte!
  Here comes a cadenza, now for a trill,
and wash those worries away.

Tomorrow

The sun'll come out tomorrow,
bet your bottom dollar that tomorrow
 there'll be sun!
Jus' thinkin' about tomorrow
clears away the cobwebs and the sorrow,
 till there's none.
When I'm stuck with a day that's grey and lonely
I just stick out my chin and grin and say:
Oh the sun'll come out tomorrow,
so you got to hang on till tomorrow
 come what may,
Tomorrow, tomorrow, I love ya tomorrow,
you're always a day away.

Thank you for the music

I'm nothing special, in fact I'm a bit of a bore,
if I tell a joke you've probably heard it before.
But I have a talent, a wonderful thing,
'cos ev'ryone listens when I start to sing,
I'm so grateful and proud,
all I want is to sing it out loud.
 So I say:
 Thank you for the music, the songs I'm singing,
 thanks for all the joy I'm bringing.
 Who can live without it?
 I ask in all honesty, what would life be,
 without a song or dance what are we?
 So I say:
 Thank you for the music, for giving it to me.

Mother says I was a dancer before I could walk,
she says I began to sing long before I could talk.
And I've often wondered, how did it all start,
who found out that nothing can capture a heart
like a melody can?
Well whoever it was, I'm a fan.
 So I say …

I've been so lucky
either I am the girl with golden hair,
 or   I have a gift I want to share,
 I wanna sing it out to ev'rybody,
 what a joy, what a life, what a chance!
 So I say …

The disco beat

There's a song in my heart and a rhythm in my feet,
gonna sing and dance to the disco beat.
I can feel it in my fingers, feel it in my toes,
it's the one way of moving that ev'ryone knows.
 So move with the beat, feel that syncopation,
 move those feet, what's the hesitation?
 Leave those cares and worries behind,
 get with the music, let your body unwind.

Do you feel in the mood, are you ready to begin?
Shake your body loose as the lights grow dim.
Hear the music all around you, moving you along,
let your feet take you dancing and join in our song.
 So move with the beat …

Whistle down the wind

Whistle down the wind, let your voices carry,
drown out all the rain,
light a patch of darkness, treacherous and scary.

Howl at the stars, whisper when you're sleeping,
I'll be there to hold you,
I'll be there to stop the chills and all the weeping.

Make it clear and strong so the whole night long,
ev'ry signal that you send until the very end,
I will not abandon you my precious friend
so try and stem the tide.
Then you'll raise a banner, send a flare up in the sky,
try to burn a torch and try to build a bonfire,
ev'ry signal that you send
until the very end I'm there.
 So whistle down the wind
 for I have always been right here.

Make it clear and strong …
 So whistle down the wind
 for I have always been right there.

The last dinosaur

Way back in a time when the earth was quite new,
giant sea monsters swam, mighty pterosaurs flew.
And the first of my fam'ly set foot on this land,
where they left ancient footprints right here on the sand.
 Now I'm the last dinosaur, I'm all alone,
 for millions of years we have called this our home.
 But now we must leave, for our time it is through,
 And they left me behind just to prove it's all true!

We wandered in forests of horsetail and fern
though our meat-eating friends gave us cause for concern,
for although we looked fierce, we were shy and refined,
and like true vegetarians quite gentle and kind.
 Now I'm the last dinosaur …

Cretaceous, Jurassic, Triassic, they say
were the times when our fossils were formed in the clay.
When my story is over don't sigh or despair.
Put me in a museum and visit me there.
 Now I'm the last dinosaur …

Man and horse

Man and horse, who'd have guessed
this would be a great success?
Man and horse, what a pair!
Found they had so much to share.
Man knew just what he was after,
something bigger, something faster,
if he could avoid the kick,
maybe this would do the trick!

Years passed by, then with pride
man discovered he could ride.
Learnt to jump, learnt to trot,
both seemed happy with their lot.
Put a saddle round its middle,
used its tail to play the fiddle.
Man was so delighted he
wanted all the world to see.

Man and horse, what an act,
came to make a life-long pact.
Man and horse, what a dream,
made a most effective team.
Pulling ploughs and herding cattle,
riding bravely into battle.
Man encouraged by his skill,
carved a horse upon the hill.

Any dream will do

I closed my eyes,
 drew back the curtain
 to see for certain
what I thought I knew.
Far, far away
 someone was weeping,
 but the world was sleeping,
any dream will do.

I wore my coat
 with golden lining,
 bright colours shining,
wonderful and new.
And in the east
 the dawn was breaking,
 the world was waiting,
any dream will do.

A crash of drums, a flash of light,
my golden cloak flew out of sight,
The colours faded into darkness, I was left alone.

May I return
 to the beginning?
 The light is dimming
and the dream is too.
The world and I,
 we are still waiting,
 still hesitating,
any dream will do.

Give me my coloured coat,
my amazing coloured coat.

Camelot

 Beneath the grassy mound,
 a mighty king now sleeps,
 in peace at last this noble warrior lies.
 And though we cannot know
 each secret that he keeps,
 the legend of King Arthur never dies.

Each noble knight so gallant and brave
 vowed to serve his king,
and fought for truth and honour
 and the glory they would bring.
Across the land they travelled
 to do their knightly deeds,
To rescue damsels in distress
 upon their mighty steeds.
And the knights came riding, riding, riding,
 armour shining in the sun.
Banners flying, maidens sighing,
 bound for Camelot, their battles won.

With thund'ring hooves and jingling spurs,
 sword and shield in hand,
in Arthur's name they ventured
 to bring peace throughout the land.
Each quest they met with courage,
 each tournament with skill,
and Avalon remains the place
 where Arthur slumbers still.
And the knights …

Turn on your video

Turn on your video,
 see how the numbers glow!
Fast forward, watch it race,
 fast forward, watch this space!
Places where you've never been,
people you have never seen
are there upon your screen
 with a video, watch it go.

We would like to travel to a place that's far away,
see the ancient sights of Athens or the traffic in L.A.
We could venture on safari, see a temple in Tibet,
though we know it's not the real thing,
 this is close as we can get!
Turn on your video …

We have always longed to see the creatures of the deep,
and the animals who wake to play when we are fast asleep.
We would love to ride a camel through the desert hot and dry,
take a trip across the mountains
 where the golden eagles fly.
Turn on your video …

Could you face the perils of a journey back in time?
From the mighty Brontosaurus to Victoria in her prime.
Climb aboard with Walter Raleigh, dance a jig with
 Anne Boleyn,
simply choose your destination,
 are you ready to begin?
Turn on your video …

Spare the rod

Wash your hands and clean your face,
hush when Master takes his place.
Pay attention, stand up straight,
don't be cheeky, don't be late!

1 | *Matthew, Mark and Luke and John,*
 | *bless the bed that I lie on.*
 | *Keep me safely through the night,*
 | *till I wake at morning light.*

2 | *Fourteen hundred and ninety two,*
 | *Columbus sailed the ocean blue.*
 | *The Normans invaded in ten sixty six*
 | *when William the Conqu'ror was up to his tricks.*

3 | *Do soh soh mi re la re,*
 | *ti re soh soh soh doh doh.*
 | *Do soh soh mi re la re,*
 | *ti re soh soh soh doh doh.*

4 | *One eight is eight, two eights are sixteen,*
 | *three eights are twenty four, four eights are thirty two.*
 | *One nine is nine, two nines are eighteen,*
 | *three nines are twenty sev'n, four nines are thirty six.*

Education makes us strong,
teaching children right from wrong.
In your lessons take a pride,
spare the rod and spoil the child!

| *Matthew … Fourteen … Do soh … One eight …*

Check each day for spots or lumps,
scarlet fever, measles, mumps,
God will put us to the test,
we can only do our best!

| *Matthew … Fourteen … Do soh … One eight …*

Stars, hide your fires

Who can say what lies ahead?
Darkest thoughts may spin their thread.
Webs of treason snared Macbeth,
bringing fear and bringing death.
Stars, hide your fires
from black and deep desires,
listen not to sisters three,
promises were not to be.
Greed and envy, you will find,
soon begin to twist the mind!

What may one brief candle show
in the shadow of its glow?
Wildest dreams and nightmares deep,
guilt and fear disturb all sleep.
Stars, hide your fires …

Treason here has shown his face,
heroes too can fall from grace.
This sad tale at last complete,
now the drum has ceased to beat.
Stars, hide your fires …

Beware the Ides of March

Beware the Ides of March, conspiracy is stirring,
beware the Ides of March, what mischief in the air.
Such murmurings and mutt'rings in shadows dark and deep,
and evil plans are whispered while Caesar tries to sleep.

Beware the Ides of March, now Cassius has spoken,
beware the Ides of March, for surely blood will flow.
All friendship will be tested, all prophecy fulfilled
when destiny is followed and Caesar's heart is stilled.

Feel the earth is trembling and groaning,
see the graves have yielded their dead.
Hear the mighty wind is a-moaning,
shooting stars to heaven have fled!

Beware the Ides of March, conspiracy is stirring …

Gently the river

1 | Gently and smoothly the river flows by,

2 | On it meanders 'neath summer's bright sky.

3 | Little fish are dancing, little fish are playing,
little fish are moving where the shadows lie.

4 | Leaping by the waterfall, hiding 'neath the
reeds so tall.

Rush-hour round

1 | What a rush as I run for the bus! And it's

2 | Beep, beep, beep, beep, out of my way!

3 | Can I get a seat please? I'm on my knees.

4 | Standing room only, ding, ding, ding, ding!

Wheels!

There were roadworks on the roundabout
and a contraflow ahead,
there were tailbacks for miles
and each traffic light was red.
So we tried out a shortcut
'cos we just couldn't wait,
but we met with a dust-cart,
that is why we were late!

1 | *Water mains, gas leaks, strikes and delays,*
dust-carts and milk-floats to get in your way.
Traffic lights, signals, roadworks ahead,
at this rate you'd better stay tucked up in bed!

2 | *Wheels go over, wheels go underneath the ground,*
slowly, quickly, wheels are always turning round.
Wheels on lorries, wheels on taxicab and tram,
ev'ry rush hour wheels are stuck in traffic jam!

3 | *With each revolution*
we find there's more pollution.
We know there's one solution:
to use our feet instead!

When we got to the station
we had time to spare,
but there seemed to be a problem,
there were people ev'rywhere.
Ev'ry train had been cancelled
and the screens all turned black,
then there came an announcement:
there were leaves on the track!

| *Water mains … Wheels go … With each revolution …*

We arrived at the bus stop
and stood in a queue,
then we waited some time
for the number thirty two.
When the driver appeared
he explained with a curse:
This bus goes no further
'cos a water main's burst!

| *Water mains … Wheels go … With each revolution …*

Grand canals

They came with pick and shovel
for to work upon the land,
from far and near they travelled
for the wages in their hand.
They came to dig and cut and build,
these strong and hardy men,
and the grand canals of England
started life in eighteen ten.

The work was hard, the day was long,
but steadily it grew,
and water flowed from spring and stream
to make the dream come true.
The bridges built, the locks complete,
the high embankments made,
and now at last the barges journeyed
down to ply their trade.

Carrying lime, carrying stone, weighed with sand and clay,
pulled by sturdy horses they would slowly make their way.
Carrying coke, carrying coal, laden with supplies,
oh, it was a wondrous sight to see a barge go by!

Across each bridge and aqueduct
the great canal did wend,
and past each farm and quarry,
as the path would gently bend.
So greetings were exchanged
at every lock and wharf and quay,
for the grand canals of England
were a friendly place to be!

The water lilies flowered
when the summer days grew long,
and water hen and coot were heard
to swell the evening song.
But still the barges travelled
through the valleys every day,
across the rolling countryside
they slowly made their way.

Carrying lime, carrying stone …

But now along this great canal
'tis only ghosts you'll hear,
though phantom barges drift from sight
if you should wander near.
A horse's hooves may echo 'neath
the bridges late at night,
and the memories come flooding back
to fill you with delight.

Carrying lime, carrying stone …

Rocking

1 | We're on the merry-go-round,
up, down, galloping round.
Waving to friends in the crowd,
music is playing so loud.

2 | On a rocking horse, easy as we go,
on a rocking horse, gentle and slow.
On a rocking horse, swaying to and fro,
on a rocking horse, gentle and slow.

3 | I shall win the race on my hobby horse,
See how fast I race: catch me if you can!
How I love to play on my hobby horse,
I'll be first away: catch me if you can!

4 | Look out! He's right behind you,
poor old Dobbin's tumbled again.
Four legs are very funny
here at the pantomime.

Steam train

From break of day to sunset we must
follow the track,
never look back,
and as we cross the countryside
we toe the line,
arrive on time.

Ooh we got music in our heart,
ooh and a love of rock and roll.
Ooh we got power in our wheels
and rhythm in our soul.

The services we offer are the
very best,
never a rest.
You'll see the steam a-flying when
the pressure's on,
you'll hear our song.

Ooh we got music …

Water and coal, iron and steel,
fire in your belly is all you can feel,
wait for the flag, whistle will blow,
open the throttle and let yourself go!

The engine gleams, the fire burns bright, we
thunder along,
noble and strong.
We love it when our pistons start
to oscillate,
accelerate.

Ooh we got music …

From break of day to sunset …

Ooh we got music …